Maths Problem solving ACTIVITY Cards

BOOK 2

Ages 8–13 • Lijun Guan

Title:	Maths Problem Solving: Activity Cards Book 2
Author:	Lijun Guan
Editor:	Tanya Tremewan
Designer:	Freshfield Design Limited
Book code:	PB00082
ISBN:	978-1-908735-62-1
Published:	2012
Publisher:	TTS Group Ltd
	Park Lane Business Park Kirkby-in-Ashfield Notts, NG17 9GU Tel: 0800 318 686 Fax: 0800 137 525
Websites:	www.tts-shopping.com
Copyright:	Text: © Lijun Guan, 2009 Edition and illustrations: ©TTS Group Ltd, 2012
About the author:	Lijun Guan's first 30 years were spent in China. As a top student in almost every subject, she adored school and chose teaching as her career so that she could stay at school for life. Retraining in New Zealand wasn't easy but now, as a fully registered primary school teacher, she gives sincere thanks to God for giving her knowledge of two languages and wisdom from understanding two cultures. This series is just one result of her desire to work as a bridge to introduce the best things from each culture to the other.
Acknowledgements:	I would like to thank my parents for helping me with childcare while I worked on this series. Thanks to my school principal Michelle Bacon, who unfortunately can't read this any more, for trusting me with the CWSA maths group in Rutherford Primary School, from which I got the idea of publishing these resources. Finally I thank Kathryn Yearsley, for helping me proofread the manuscripts. Without them, these books might not have been possible.

Photocopy notice:

Permission is given to schools and teachers who buy this book to reproduce it (and/or any extracts) by photocopying or otherwise, but only for use at their present school. Copies may not be supplied to anyone else or made or used for any other purpose.

Contents

Introduction

52. Tunnel test
53. Number triangle
54. Sums for the squares
55. Make it true (1)
56. Make it true (2)
57. The 20th shape
58. Perching birds
59. Fruity survey
60. Sum to 10
61. Letters for numbers
62. The mystery of 7
63. One-stroke drawing
64. Future ages
65. How old is the old man?
66. Rabbits and mushrooms
67. Poor old frog
68. Chocolate prize
69. Time to cross the river
70. Going to school
71. Kayaking
72. What day will it be?
73. Hanging lanterns
74. 100 hours later
75. Don't move the trees
76. Divide the garden
77. Eight 8s
78. Which is bigger?
79. How many elephants?
80. How many corners?
81. Just enough fertiliser
82. Apples in bags
83. Safe keys
84. Same sum and product
85. Cut the cake
86. Move the matchsticks
87. Equal work
88. In the swimming pool
89. Superhero swap
90. Strawberry jam
91. Look at the pattern
92. Find the rule
93. Sweets in the circles
94. Half of the people
95. A town and a city
96. Visit to the zoo
97. Puzzling families
98. Not in our club
99. What are the 3 numbers?
100. The missing weight
101. Take away 1 matchstick
102. Time to meet

Introduction

In life, we are constantly faced with the need to solve problems or make decisions based on reasoning. These skills can be improved by training: the more we try, the better we will be. *Maths Problem Solving* is a series designed to provide some of this training. Although the immediate focus of the problems is on mathematical skills and the maths curriculum, they have far wider relevance in guiding the next generation to become better problem solvers and decision makers.

Each problem is presented on its own task card and has an accompanying solution card. The solution cards are a central part of the process as these problems tend to work best when children feel they have support on hand if they need it. I recommend presenting photocopies of the problem and its solution together for independent work (eg, for early finishers). In this way, children can gain enjoyment from discovering the answer to a problem that they found so hard to solve: "Wow, it's just like that! Why didn't I think of that?" In addition, looking at the answer allows them to learn how to solve a certain type of problem and follow a similar thinking process in the future.

Alternatively or as well, these problems are effective with children who have high ability or interest in maths, especially problem solving, or enjoy challenging themselves. In this case, the teacher might guide the children as they work through the problems.

I hope the children in your class have as much fun with these problems as I had with similar types of problems in China 30 years ago. The level of enthusiasm from children with whom I have trialled them is amazing. And many of them come up with novel solutions that I have never even thought of.

© TTS Group Ltd, 2012

CARD 52: **Tunnel test** — PROBLEM

Mum and Dad take their two boys for an outdoor adventure. When they get to a tunnel where only one person can go through at a time, the two boys start arguing about who should be the first one to go through.

Dad laughs and says, "I will give you a test. Whoever gets it right can go through first." He throws a coin and it lands heads up. Then Dad asks, "Will it be heads up or tails up after we turn it around 2,009 times?" One of the boys says heads and the other one says tails.

Who do you think should go through the tunnel first?

© TTS Group Ltd, 2012

CARD 52: **Tunnel test** — SOLUTION

The boy who says tails should go through first. The first time they turn the coin, it will be tails up, the second time heads, the third time tails, the fourth time heads … So all the odd numbers will be tails and all the even numbers will be heads. 2,009 is an odd number so after 2,009 turns it will be tails.

© TTS Group Ltd, 2012

CARD 53: **Number triangle** — PROBLEM

Put 1, 2, 3, 4, 5 and 6 into the following circles to make the sum of the 3 numbers on each side equal 9.

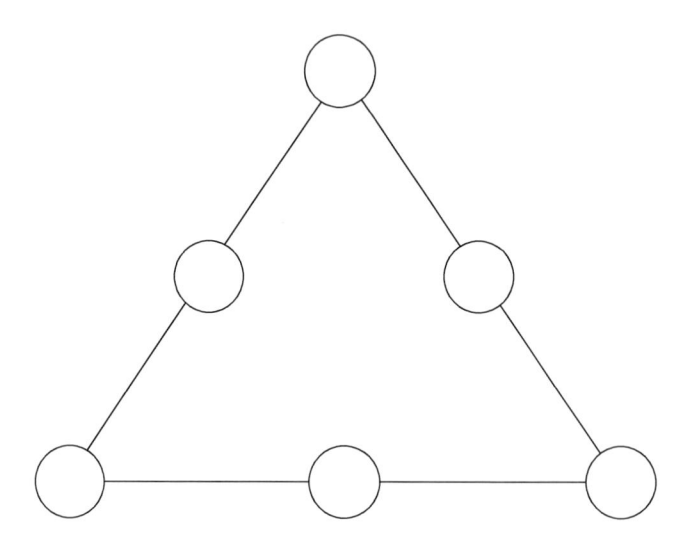

CARD 53: **Number triangle** — SOLUTION

The sum of numbers 1, 2, 3, 4, 5 and 6 is 21. If the three numbers on each side add up to 9, the sum of all three sides should be 27. To get a total of 27, each of the numbers in the 3 corners has been used twice.

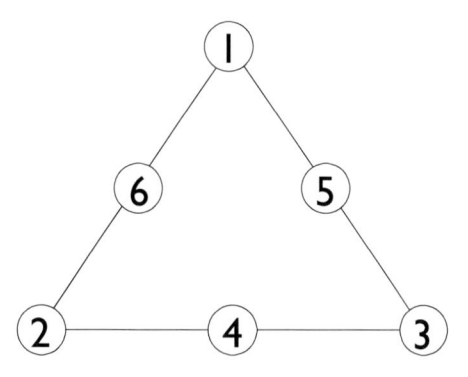

To find the sum of the 3 numbers in the corners, we work out 27 − 21 = 6. The only possible combination of 3 numbers to get the total of 6 is 1 + 2 + 3. So the numbers in the corners must be 1, 2 and 3. Once you put these numbers in the corners, working out the other numbers is easy.

CARD 54: **Sums for the squares** — PROBLEM

Fill in any numbers (except 0) in the boxes to make the sum of each side of the square equal 5 and the sum of all the numbers on all sides equal 12.

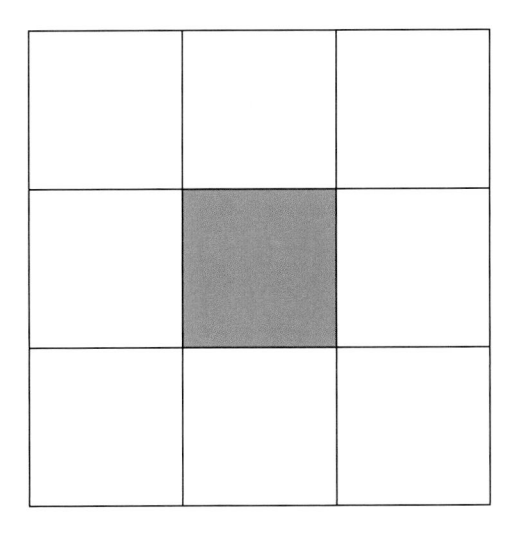

© TTS Group Ltd, 2012

CARD 54: **Sums for the squares** — SOLUTION

To make 3 numbers (except 0) add up to 5, we can only use either 3 + 1 + 1 or 2 + 2 + 1. Because the sum of each side is 5, the sum of the numbers on four sides is 20. We find out the sum of the four numbers in the corners from 20 − 12 = 8. So the possible combination of numbers in the corners is either 2, 2, 2, 2 or 3, 3, 1, 1. If you put either combination in the corners, you can easily work out the numbers in between. (Both options are correct.)

2	1	2
1		1
2	1	2

3	1	1
1		1
1	1	3

© TTS Group Ltd, 2012

CARD 55: **Make it true (1)** — PROBLEM

Change **one** of the plus (+) signs to an equals (=) sign so that you create an addition problem with a true answer.

1 + 2 + 3 + 4 + 5 + 6 + 7 + 8 + 9 + 10 + 11 + 12 + 13 + 14 + 15 + 16 + 17 + 18 + 19 + 20

CARD 55: **Make it true (1)** — SOLUTION

1 + 2 + 3 + 4 + 5 + 6 + 7 + 8 + 9 + 10 + 11 + 12 + 13 + 14 = 15 + 16 + 17 + 18 + 19 + 20

The sum of numbers 1 to 20 is 210. Half of 210 is 105 so each side should sum to 105. As we find that 20 + 19 + 18 + 17 + 16 + 15 = 105, we need to change the plus sign after 14 into an equals sign.

CARD 56: **Make it true (2)** — PROBLEM

Add in **two** plus (+) signs and **two** minus (−) signs to make the answer true.

$$1\ 2\ 3\ 4\ 5\ 6\ 7\ 8\ 9 = 100$$

CARD 56: **Make it true (2)** — SOLUTION

$$123 + 4 - 5 + 67 - 89 = 100$$

© TTS Group Ltd, 2012

CARD 57: **The 20th shape** — PROBLEM

Jim and Amy found their way through a maze. When they finally reached the exit, they found the door was tightly shut. Beside the door was a note that said, "The door will only open if you can tell – in 1 minute or less – what the 20th shape will be in each pattern." Jim and Amy had a look and drew the 20th shape for each pattern. Then the door opened automatically and they got out of the maze.

Work out the 20th shape on each line to see if you could get out of the maze too.

1. ▲ ● ▲ ● ▲ ● ▲ ●
2. ■ ◆ ☻ ■ ◆ ☻ ■ ◆ ☻ ■ ◆ ☻
3. ▲ ● ▲ ☻ ▲ ● ▲ ☻ ▲ ● ▲ ☻

CARD 57: **The 20th shape** — SOLUTION

1. The pattern starts repeating after 2 shapes. As 20 ÷ 2 = 10, the 20th shape is the last shape of the 10th repetition of the pattern: a circle ●.
2. The pattern repeats every three shapes. As 20 ÷ 3 = 6 r 2, the 20th shape is the second shape after the 6th repetition: a diamond ◆.
3. The pattern repeats every four shapes. As 20 ÷ 4 = 5, the 20th pattern is the last shape of the 5th repetition: a smiley face ☻.

CARD 58: **Perching birds** — PROBLEM

There are 24 birds sitting on 3 trees. After 4 birds fly from the first tree to the second tree and 5 birds fly from the second tree to the third tree, the number of birds on each tree becomes the same.

Do you know how many birds were originally on each tree?

© TTS Group Ltd, 2012

CARD 58: **Perching birds** — SOLUTION

Originally there were 12 birds on the first tree, 9 birds on the second tree and 3 birds on the third tree.

As 24 ÷ 3 = 8, we know that there are 8 birds on each tree when the number becomes the same. 4 birds fly away from the first tree so there were 12 birds there originally (12 − 4 = 8). Those 4 birds flew to the second tree but 5 birds also flew away from the second tree so there were 9 birds originally (9 + 4 − 5 = 8). As the third tree gets 8 birds by gaining 5 extra birds, there were 3 birds originally (3 + 5 = 8).

© TTS Group Ltd, 2012

CARD 59 : **Fruity survey** — PROBLEM

Amber does a survey of her class. She finds 12 of her 30 classmates like bananas, 8 of them like strawberries and 3 of them like both bananas and strawberries.

How many of her classmates like neither bananas nor strawberries?

CARD 59 : **Fruity survey** — SOLUTION

13 of Amber's classmates like neither bananas nor strawberries.

If we take away the people who like bananas and people who like strawberries from the total number of people in the class (30), we take away the people who like bananas and strawberries twice. So if we then add the number of people who like both bananas and strawberries (3), we get the number of people who don't like either bananas or strawberries: $30 - 12 - 8 + 3 = 13$.

CARD 60: **Sum to 10** — PROBLEM

Put 1, 2, 3, 4, 5, 6 or 7 in each circle to make the sum of each line equal 10. You may use each number only once.

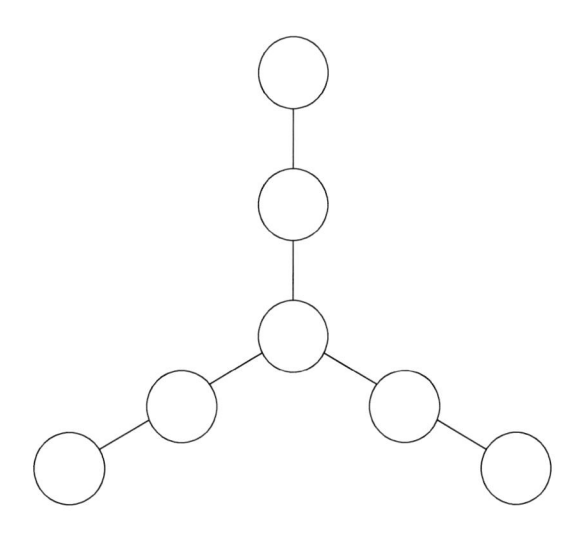

CARD 60: **Sum to 10** — SOLUTION

There are 3 lines and the numbers on each line must add up to 10. So the sums of the numbers on all 3 lines is 30, if we count the number in the middle circle twice more as it has to be used twice more than the other numbers. The sum of 1, 2, 3, 4, 5, 6 and 7 is 28.

As we need to add the number in the middle circle twice more to reach the total of 30, the number in the middle circle can only be 1. Once you have decided the number in the middle circle, it is easy to work out the numbers in the other circles.

CARD 61 : **Letters for numbers** — PROBLEM

Each different letter below stands for a different number. The number may be any digit from 0 to 9 (including both these numbers).

Can you work out what each letter stands for? (Note that the number 1 is already included.)

$$\begin{array}{r} 1\,A\,B\,C\,D\,E \\ \times \qquad\qquad 3 \\ \hline A\,B\,C\,D\,E\,1 \end{array}$$

CARD 61 : **Letters for numbers** — SOLUTION

A = 4, B = 2, C = 8, D = 5, E = 7

For 3 × E = _1, the only possibility is 3 × 7 = 21 so E = 7. For D × 3 + 2 = _7 (when we take over the 2 to the second column), the only possibility is 5 × 3 + 2 = 17 so D = 5. For C × 3 + 1 = _5, the only possibility is 8 × 3 + 1 = 25 so C = 8. For B × 3 + 2 = 8, the only possibility is 2 × 3 + 2 = 8 so B = 2. For A × 3 = _2, the only possibility is 4 × 3 = 12 so A = 4. The first digit 1 × 3 + 1 = A also shows A = 4, which confirms that the whole process is correct.

CARD 62 : **The mystery of 7** PROBLEM

We take a number and add 7, multiply 7, take away 7 and finally divide by 7 and the result is 7.

What was the original number?

CARD 62 : **The mystery of 7** SOLUTION

The original number was 1.

We can find the number by reversing the order of the operations:

1. What number divided by 7 makes 7? 49
2. What number take away 7 makes 49? 56
3. What number times 7 makes 56? 8
4. What number plus 7 makes 8? 1

CARD 63 : **One-stroke drawing** — PROBLEM

Can you draw each of the following drawings in one stroke (without stopping in the middle or going back over any part)? If so, do a drawing to show how.

1. 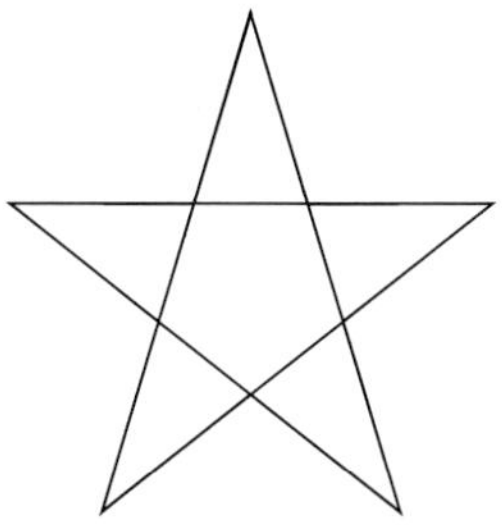
2.
3.

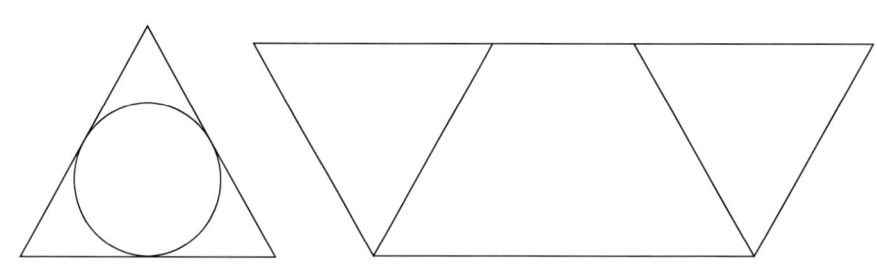

CARD 63 : **One-stroke drawing** — SOLUTION

One-stroke drawings are possible for shapes 1 and 2 but not 3.

1. 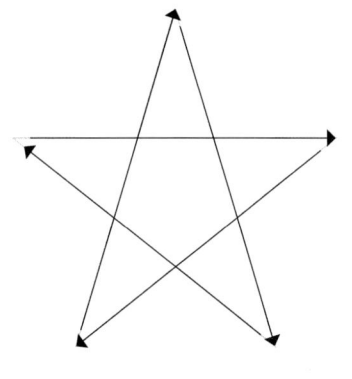
2.

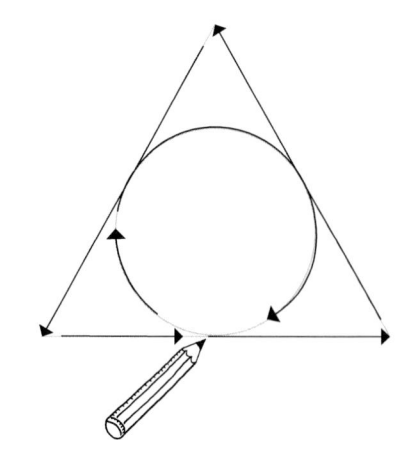

CARD 64 : **Future ages** — PROBLEM

Dawn is 12 and her brother is 8. How old will Dawn be and how old will her brother be when the sum of their ages is 40?

CARD 64 : **Future ages** — SOLUTION

Dawn's brother will be 18 and she will be 22.

The sum of their ages now is 20. For the sum of their ages to be 40, we need to add 20 years to their ages now in total, which means we add 10 years to each person's age now.

CARD 65 : **How old is the old man?** — PROBLEM

An old man says if you add 12 to his age, then divide by 4, then take away 15, then multiply the answer by 10, the answer will be 100.

Do you know how old the old man is now?

© TTS Group Ltd, 2012

CARD 65 : **How old is the old man?** SOLUTION

He is 88 years old. You can find out his age by reversing the operations and doing them in reverse order:

1. $100 \div 10 = 10$
2. $10 + 15 = 25$
3. $25 \times 4 = 100$
4. $100 - 12 = 88$

© TTS Group Ltd, 2012

CARD 66: **Rabbits and mushrooms** PROBLEM

Mother Rabbit and Baby Rabbit pick mushrooms. They each put the mushrooms they pick in their own basket. They get 160 mushrooms altogether. Then Mother eats 20 of her mushrooms and Baby picks another 10 mushrooms. Now they both have the same number of mushrooms in their baskets.

How many mushrooms did they each have in their basket when they had 160 altogether?

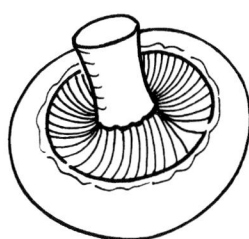

© TTS Group Ltd, 2012

CARD 66: **Rabbits and mushrooms** SOLUTION

Originally Mother Rabbit had 95 and Baby Rabbit had 65.

After Mother eats 20 of her mushrooms and Baby picks 10, they have 160 − 20 + 10 = 150 mushrooms altogether. As both of them have the same number of mushrooms now, they each have 75 mushrooms (150 ÷ 2 = 75). So Mother had 75 + 20 = 95 and Baby had 75 − 10 = 65 previously.

© TTS Group Ltd, 2012

CARD 67 : **Poor old frog** PROBLEM

An old frog falls into a well that is 10 metres deep. He can climb 3 metres up in the daytime but falls 2 metres back at night.

How many days does the poor old frog need to climb before he is out of the well?

© TTS Group Ltd, 2012

CARD 67 : **Poor old frog** SOLUTION

He must climb for 8 days. Because he goes 3 metres up and 2 metres down each day, it is the same as if he goes up 1 metre each day. So you might expect that the frog would need 10 days to get out of a well that is 10 metres deep. But on the eighth day, he would climb up 3 metres and be able to get out of the well without falling backwards.

© TTS Group Ltd, 2012

CARD 68 : **Chocolate prize** PROBLEM

A boy wins a box of chocolates as a prize. He gives half of them to his parents and then he gives half of the number of chocolates that are left over to his grandparents. He then eats 10 of the chocolates he has left, and finds he still has 10 chocolates to spare.

How many chocolates were in the box to begin with?

© TTS Group Ltd, 2012

CARD 68 : **Chocolate prize** SOLUTION

There were originally 80 chocolates in the box.

Because he ate 10 chocolates and still had another 10 after he had given the others away, he had 20 left after he gave half of the remaining chocolates to his grandparents. He therefore gave 20 chocolates to his grandparents too because that is the other half of the chocolates he had left over after he gave half to his parents. Therefore before he gave any chocolates to his grandparents, he had 40 chocolates. He gave half of his chocolates to his parents so, before he gave any to his parents, he had double 40 chocolates – or 80 chocolates in the full box.

© TTS Group Ltd, 2012

CARD 69 : **Time to cross the river** — PROBLEM

A group of 49 explorers is trying to cross a river. There is only 1 raft available and it can hold 7 people. It takes 3 minutes to get to the other side of the river.

How long will it take for the whole team to cross the river?

CARD 69 : **Time to cross the river** — SOLUTION

It will take 45 minutes.

Because 1 person is always needed to row the raft back except for the last time, only 6 people can cross the river every 6 minutes (allowing for a return journey). After 7 groups of 6 people are across in this way, 42 people have crossed the river in 42 minutes. There are 7 people left. They can get to the other side in a one-way crossing without returning the raft. So we just add on another 3 minutes.

CARD 70 : **Going to school** — PROBLEM

Hannah and her brother leave home at the same time to go to Rutherford School. Hannah walks 60 metres per minute and her brother walks 90 metres per minute. When Hannah's brother gets to school, he realises he has left his school bag at home. So he turns around and starts to walk back home. He meets Hannah on the way back, when he is 180 metres away from school.

What is the distance between Hannah's home and Rutherford School?

© TTS Group Ltd, 2012

CARD 70 : **Going to school** — SOLUTION

Hannah's home is 900 metres away from Rutherford School.

Every minute Hannah's brother walks 30 metres more than Hannah. When Hannah's brother meets her on his way back, after getting to school first and then walking another 180 metres, he has walked 2 × 180 = 360 metres further than Hannah. So we know they have walked for 360 ÷ 30 = 12 minutes. As we also know Hannah's walking speed is 60 metres per minute, we know that over 12 minutes she walks 12 × 60 = 720 metres. She still has 180 metres to go. As 720 + 180 = 900 metres, we know her home is 900 metres away from school.

© TTS Group Ltd, 2012

CARD 71 : **Kayaking** — PROBLEM

44 children go kayaking. They have 10 kayaks between them. The big kayaks can hold 6 people each and the small kayaks can hold 4 people each.

How many big kayaks and how many small kayaks do they have if there are just enough spaces for all the children?

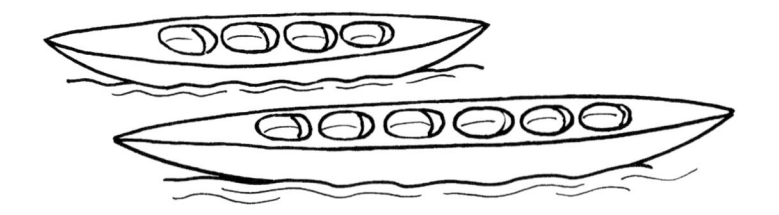

© TTS Group Ltd, 2012

CARD 71 : **Kayaking** — SOLUTION

They have 2 big kayaks and 8 small kayaks.

If all 10 kayaks were big, they could hold 60 children and there would be 16 more spaces (60 − 44 = 16) than they need. Each big kayak can hold 2 more people than a small kayak. As 16 ÷ 2 = 8, we know that if they use 8 small kayaks and 2 big kayaks, there will be just enough space for all the 44 children.

© TTS Group Ltd, 2012

CARD 72 : What day will it be? — PROBLEM

If it is Wednesday today, what day will it be 100 days later?

CARD 72 : What day will it be? — SOLUTION

It will be a Friday. There are 7 days in each week. As 100 ÷ 7 = 14 r 2, we know that if it is Wednesday today, after 98 days it will still be Wednesday because 14 multiplied by 7 is 98. But we want to know the day 100 days later — 2 days after Wednesday, which is Friday.

CARD 73 : **Hanging lanterns**   PROBLEM

Chelsea is helping to hang some lanterns in the school hall for a concert. She hangs 3 red lanterns, then 2 blue lanterns and then 1 yellow lantern, and then continues with this pattern.

What colour will the 40th lantern be?

CARD 73 : **Hanging lanterns**   SOLUTION

The 40th lantern will be blue.

We can see the pattern repeats every 6 lanterns (3 + 2 + 1 = 6). As 40 ÷ 6 = 6 r 4, we know that the 40th lantern is the 4th lantern after 6 repeating patterns. After the first 3 red lanterns, the 4th one is blue. So that is the colour of the 40th lantern.

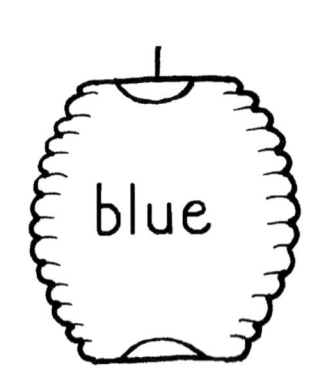

CARD 76 : **Divide the garden**   PROBLEM

Mrs White asks her 5 children to weed her square garden. In her garden is a little square pool (see the picture on the right). She divides her garden into 5 areas of the same size for each child to work on. How does she do that?

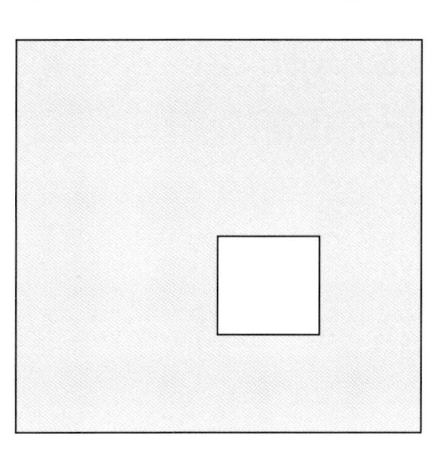

CARD 76 : **Divide the garden**   SOLUTION

She divides her garden into areas A, B, C, D and E as shown on the right. No one needs to do gardening in the pond so that is not included in anyone's area.

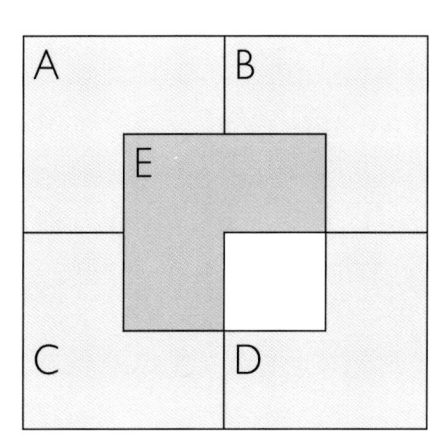

CARD 77: **Eight 8s** — PROBLEM

Can you use eight 8s to make 5 numbers that we can add together to make 1,000?

CARD 77: **Eight 8s** — SOLUTION

888 + 88 + 8 + 8 + 8 = 1,000

888 is the closest number to 1,000 that we can make with 8s. 888 is 112 less than 1,000. If we add 88 to 888, we still need 24 to make 1,000 because 112 − 88 = 24. That helps us complete our sum because 24 is the sum of three single 8s.

CARD 78 : **Which is bigger?** — PROBLEM

Which is bigger:

- the sum of the numbers 1, 2, 3, 4, 5, 6, 7, 8, 9 and 0

  or

- the product of these numbers?

CARD 78 : **Which is bigger?** — SOLUTION

The sum of the numbers is bigger than the product.

Normally the sum of a set of numbers is smaller than its product. However, because the number 0 is included in the calculations, the product becomes 0. So the sum of this set of numbers is bigger than the product.

CARD 79 : **How many elephants?** PROBLEM

A lonely elephant meets a herd of elephants. He says, "Hello, 100 elephants." One of the elephants in the herd answers, "There are not 100 elephants in our herd. But if we added another herd of the same number and another half of our number and another quarter of our number and you, then there would be 100 in our herd."

The lonely elephant cannot figure out how many elephants are in the herd right now. Can you help him?

© TTS Group Ltd, 2012

CARD 79 : **How many elephants?** SOLUTION

There are 36 elephants in the herd.

We know that 100 − the lonely elephant = 99. So the number of elephants + the number of the elephants + half of the number of the elephants + a quarter of the number of the elephants = 99.

If we use x to represent the number of elephants, it becomes:

$x + x + \frac{1}{2}x + \frac{1}{4}x = 99$

so $2\frac{3}{4}x = 99$

so $x = 36$

© TTS Group Ltd, 2012

CARD 80 : **How many corners?** PROBLEM

A rectangular table is standing in the room. If you cut one corner off, how many corners will the table have?

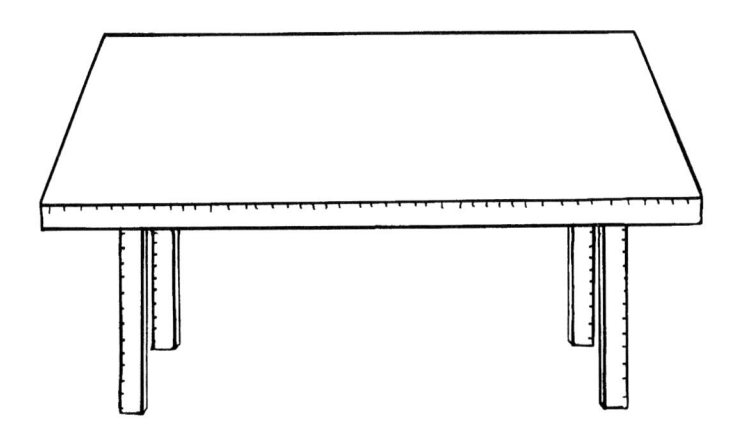

CARD 80 : **How many corners?** SOLUTION

If we cut one corner off, we create two new corners. So the table will have 5 corners after you cut off one.

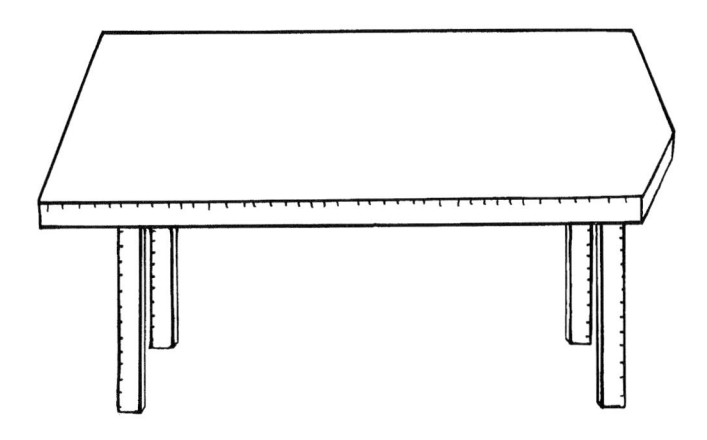

CARD 81: **Just enough fertiliser** — PROBLEM

Old McDonald keeps his organic fertiliser in a 1 litre container. He needs to put 500 ml into a spray bottle that he can use on his plants, but he has only got a 300 ml spray bottle and a 400 ml spray bottle.

How can he get the amount of organic fertiliser he needs using the spray bottles he has without using any other measuring equipment and without wasting any organic fertiliser?

© TTS Group Ltd, 2012

CARD 81: **Just enough fertiliser** — SOLUTION

One way to get 500 ml is to put 400 ml in one bottle and 100 ml in the other. Old McDonald has a spray bottle that holds 400 ml. So he pours 400 ml into the 400 ml bottle. Is there any way to get another 100 ml from the 1 litre container without using other measuring equipment?

The difference between the 400 ml bottle and the 300 ml bottle is 100 ml. So Old McDonald fills up the 300 ml bottle with organic fertiliser from the bottle that contains 400 ml of organic fertiliser. He now has 300 ml in the 300 ml bottle and 100 ml in the 400 ml bottle. He pours the 300 ml of organic fertiliser back into the 1 litre container. Then he pours the 100 ml of organic fertiliser into the 300 ml bottle. Finally he fills up the 400 ml bottle from the 1 litre container. Now Old McDonald has measured out 500 ml (400 ml + 100 ml) of organic fertiliser to use on his plants.

© TTS Group Ltd, 2012

CARD 82: **Apples in bags** — PROBLEM

Dan the shop assistant is trying to put apples into bags so that it is easier to sell them. He tries to put them into bags of 10 but one bag is short by 1 apple. Then he tries to put them into bags of 9 but still one bag is short by 1 apple. He then tries bags of 8, 7, 6, 5, 4, 3 and 2, and always finds one bag is short by 1 apple.

Can you work out how many apples Dan has?

CARD 82: **Apples in bags** — SOLUTION

Dan has 2,519 apples.

The total number of the apples is one less than the least common multiple of 2, 3, 4, 5, 6, 7, 8, 9 and 10. The least common multiple of these numbers is $7 \times 8 \times 9 \times 5 = 2{,}520$. So the number of the apples is 1 less than that: 2,519.

CARD 83 : **Safe keys** PROBLEM

There are 3 workers and 3 safes. There are 2 keys for each safe.

How can you arrange the keys so that every worker can open all the 3 safes on her own?

CARD 83 : **Safe keys** SOLUTION

Number the safes as 1, 2 and 3. Give 1 key for each safe to a different worker. Put the other key to safe 2 inside safe 1, put the other key to safe 3 inside safe 2, and put the other key to safe 1 inside safe 3.

Now the worker with a safe 1 key can open safe 2 because the key to safe 2 is inside safe 1. Once she opens safe 2, she can get key to safe 3 from there. It works in a similar way for the other 2 workers so they can all open the three safes.

CARD 84: **Same sum and product** PROBLEM

There are three numbers that we can combine to make a sum and a product that are the same.

What are the three numbers?

© TTS Group Ltd, 2012

CARD 84: **Same sum and product** SOLUTION

Normally the product of a certain combination of numbers is bigger than the sum. The bigger the numbers are, the bigger the difference between the sum and the product. Because the sum and the product are the same for these 3 numbers, we can expect them to be fairly small so we can try various combinations of small numbers.

When we try 1, 2 and 3, we find their sum is 6 and their product is 6. So the answer is 1, 2 and 3.

© TTS Group Ltd, 2012

CARD 85 : **Cut the cake** — PROBLEM

Dad makes a cake and puts 7 jellybeans on it.

Can you make 3 cuts to divide the cake into 7 pieces with a jellybean on each piece?

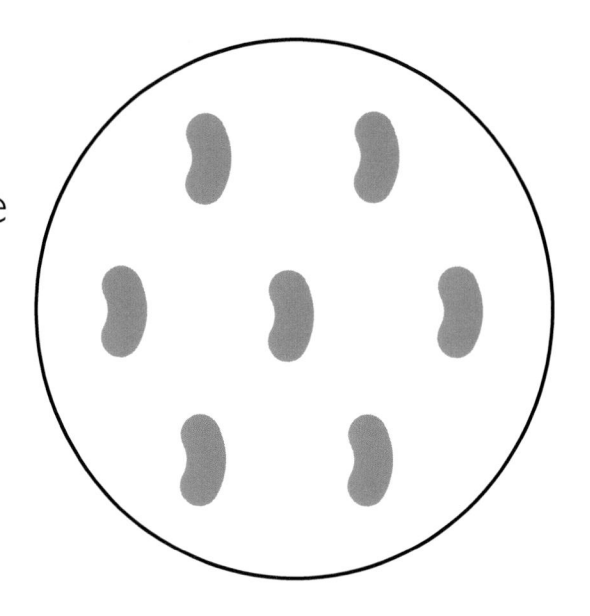

CARD 85 : **Cut the cake** — SOLUTION

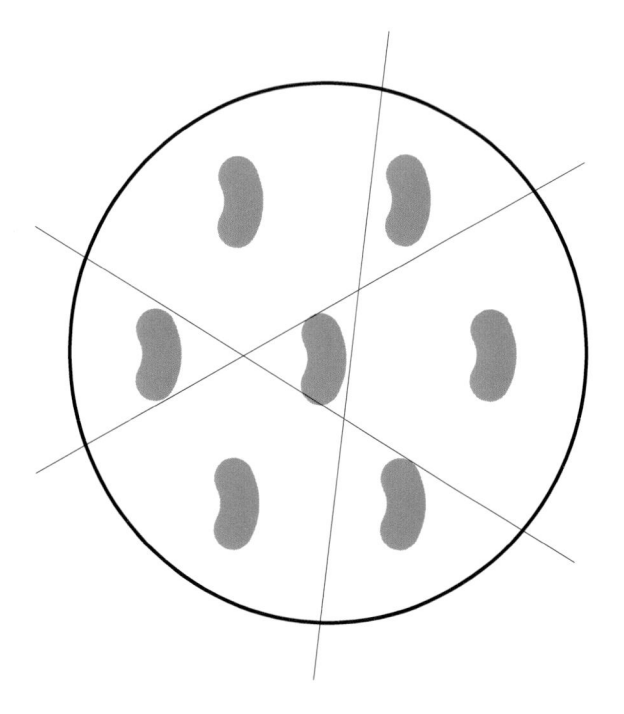

CARD 86 : **Move the matchsticks** — PROBLEM

The 7 squares below have been made with 20 matchsticks.

Can you move 3 matchsticks to make 5 squares with the same number of matchsticks?

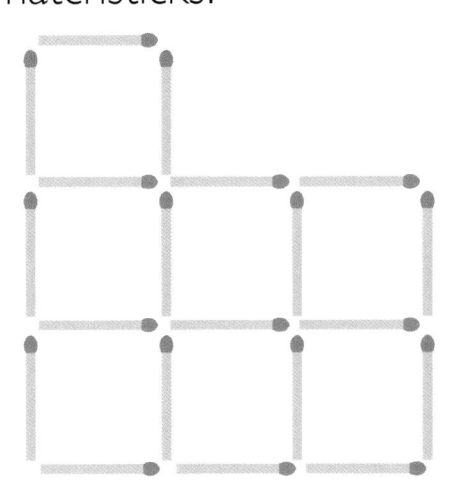

CARD 86 : **Move the matchsticks** — SOLUTION

One way to make fewer squares with the same number of matchsticks is to reduce the number of shared borders. If we are using 20 matchsticks to make 5 squares, none of the 5 squares should share its border with any other.

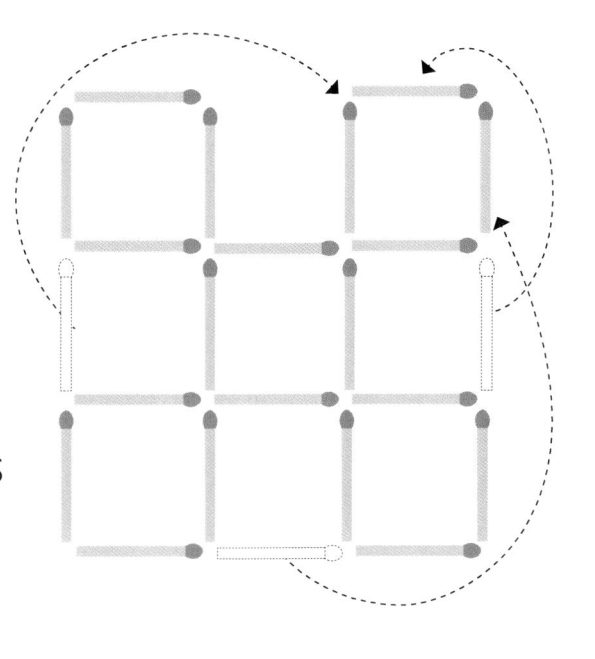

CARD 87 : Equal work — PROBLEM

Mrs Trent is trying to get Years 1, 2, 3 and 4 to take charge of their school field and make sure there is no rubbish left lying around. The picture below shows how the field is laid out.

How can she divide the field equally so that the amount of work is fair for each year?

© TTS Group Ltd, 2012

CARD 87 : Equal work — SOLUTION

Cut each square into 4 smaller squares. Based on the numbering in the picture below, Year 1 can work in squares 1, 2 and 3; Year 2 can work in squares 4, 5 and 6; Year 3 can work in squares 7, 8 and 9; and Year 4 can work in squares 10, 11 and 12.

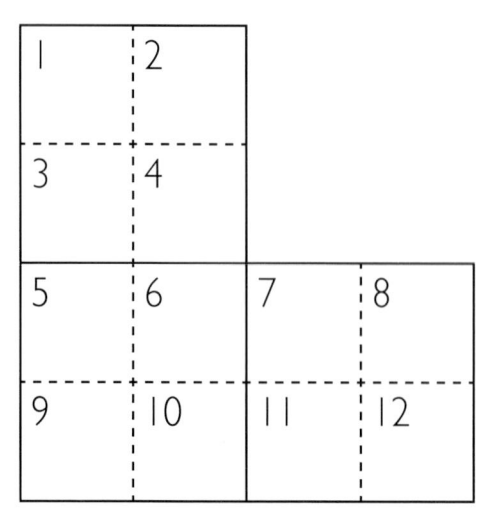

© TTS Group Ltd, 2012

CARD 88: **In the swimming pool** PROBLEM

In a swimming pool, all the boys are wearing blue swimming costumes and all the girls are wearing red swimming costumes. A boy in the pool says he can see equal numbers of blue swimming costumes and red swimming costumes. A girl in the pool says that she sees twice as many as blue swimming costumes as red swimming costumes.

Do you know how many people are in the swimming pool?

CARD 88: **In the swimming pool** SOLUTION

There are 7 people in the swimming pool: 3 girls and 4 boys.

Because a boy can see equal numbers of blue and red swimming costumes (meaning he is not counting his own), there is 1 more boy in the pool than girls. As a girl sees twice as many blue swimming costumes as red ones, we know the number of boys would be double the number of girls if there was 1 girl less. From the boy's comment, we also know that there would be 2 more boys than girls if there was 1 girl less. 2 more than the girls is the same as twice as many as the number of girls, which means the boys' number is double 2.

Combining the above information, we can conclude there are 4 boys and 4 – 1 = 3 girls, or 7 people altogether.

CARD 89 : **Superhero swap** — PROBLEM

Both John and George want to swap their superhero cards for Sophie's comic book but neither of them has enough cards. John needs 1 more card and George needs 100 more cards. But if they put their cards together, they still do not have enough cards to get the comic book.

Do you know how many cards each of them has and how many cards Sophie wants for the comic book?

© TTS Group Ltd, 2012

CARD 89 : **Superhero swap** — SOLUTION

John has 99 cards and George has none. Sophie wants 100 cards to swap for the comic book.

John only needs 1 more card but if they put their cards together they still do not have enough to get the comic book. That means George must have no cards at all. As he needs 100 cards to get the comic book, we know that Sophie must want 100 cards for it. As John has 1 card fewer than this amount, he must have 99 cards.

© TTS Group Ltd, 2012

CARD 90 : **Strawberry jam** — PROBLEM

Both John and George have grown strawberries. Mum says that if they have enough strawberries, they can make strawberry jam. Neither John nor George has enough strawberries on his own to make the jam. John needs another 3.4 kilograms of strawberries and George needs another 2.6 kilograms. But if they put their strawberries together, they would have just enough to make the jam.

Do you know the weight of strawberries each boy has grown and the weight they need to make the jam?

© TTS Group Ltd, 2012

CARD 90 : **Strawberry jam** — SOLUTION

When they combine their strawberries, the two boys have just enough to make jam so the weight of John's strawberries must be just what George needs. George needs 2.6 kilograms more strawberries so John must have 2.6 kilograms of strawberries. Likewise, the weight that John needs is what George has: 3.4 kilograms. The total is 6 kilograms, the weight they need to make strawberry jam.

© TTS Group Ltd, 2012

CARD 91: **Look at the pattern** — PROBLEM

Use the pattern to work out the number in the fifth column of the fifth row.

1   2   6   7   15   16 …

3   5   8   14   17 …

4   9   13   18 …

10   12   19 …

11   20 …

21 …

CARD 91: **Look at the pattern** — SOLUTION

Carrying on with the pattern, we can find the number in the fifth column of the fifth row.

1   2   6   7   15   16   28   29
3   5   8   14   17   27   30   44
4   9   13   18   26   31   43 …
10   12   19   25   32   42 …
11   20   24   33   **41** …
21   23   34   40 …
22   35   39 …
36   38
37

CARD 92: **Find the rule** — PROBLEM

What will the next pattern be?

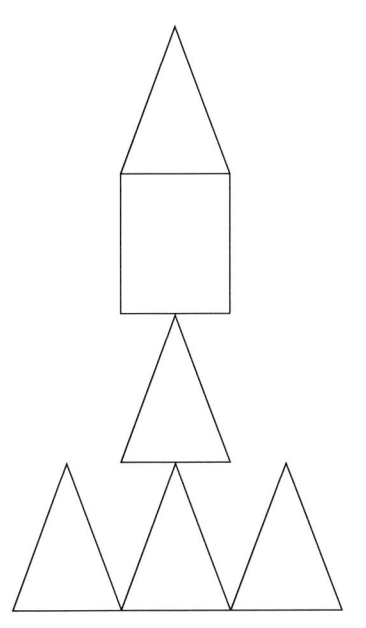

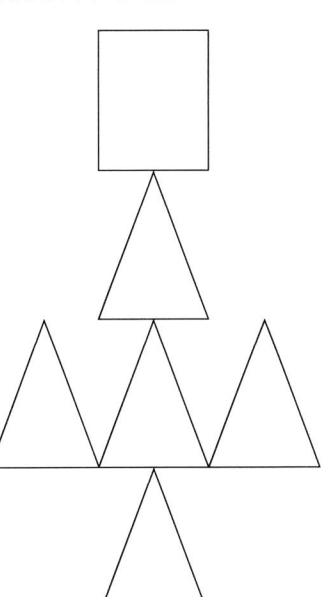

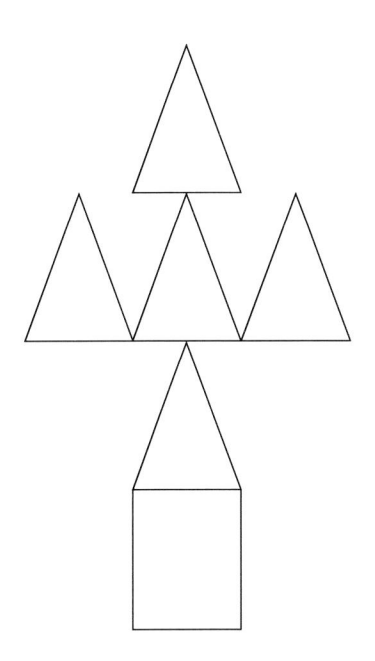

CARD 92: **Find the rule** — SOLUTION

The rule is to move the top shape to the bottom each time. So the next pattern is:

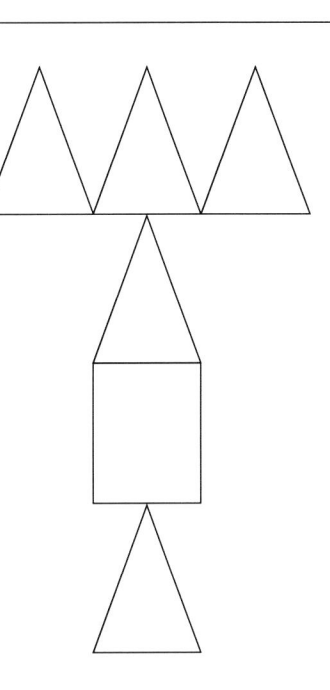

CARD 93: **Sweets in the circles** — PROBLEM

If there are 10 sweets in each circle, then how many sweets will be in these 3 circles altogether?

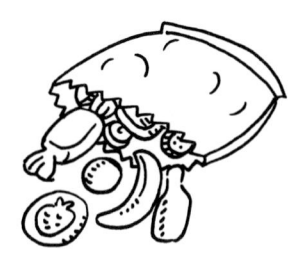

CARD 93: **Sweets in the circles** — SOLUTION

There will be 10 sweets altogether.

If you put 10 sweets in the middle of the small circle, then there will also be 10 sweets in the other circles.

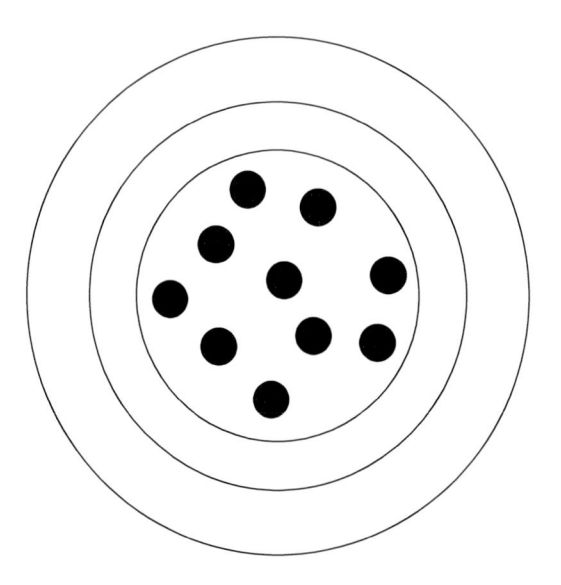

CARD 94: **Half of the people** — PROBLEM

When Mrs Morrison walks into her classroom at 9 am, she is very angry because the number of children present is only half the number of people in the room.

How many children are present when Mrs. Morrison enters her classroom?

CARD 94: **Half of the people** — SOLUTION

When Mrs Morrison enters her room, she is 1 of the people present. The number of children present is half the number of people in the room and Mrs Morrison is the other half. So there is only 1 child present.

CARD 95 : **A town and a city** — PROBLEM

Linda starts from a town and heads towards a city at a speed of 50 kilometres per hour. David starts from the city heading towards the town at a speed of 60 kilometres per hour.

Who is closer to the town when they meet each other?

CARD 95 : **A town and a city** — SOLUTION

When they meet, they are at the same point of the route. So the distance to the town is the same for both of them.

CARD 96: **Visit to the zoo** — PROBLEM

This is a map of Zale's Zoo. Can you visit all the animals in the zoo without following any of the same paths more than once?

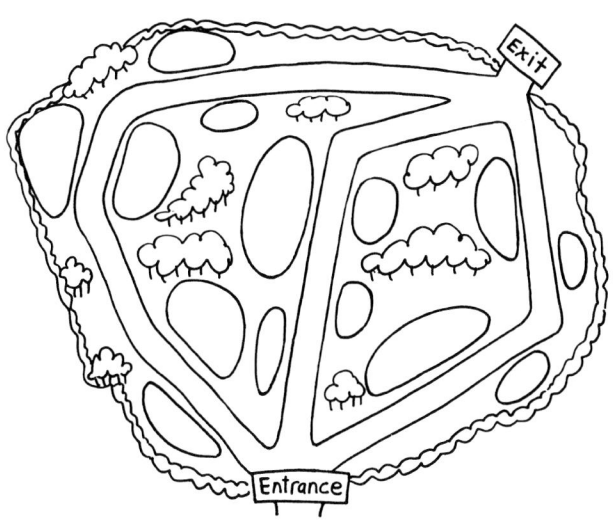

© TTS Group Ltd, 2012

CARD 96: **Visit to the zoo** — SOLUTION

Yes, you can. The zoo map can be simplified into a shape like this:

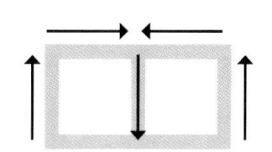

When we transfer the arrows on this shape to the zoo, we can see that you can walk around all the paths without following any of them more than once – like this:

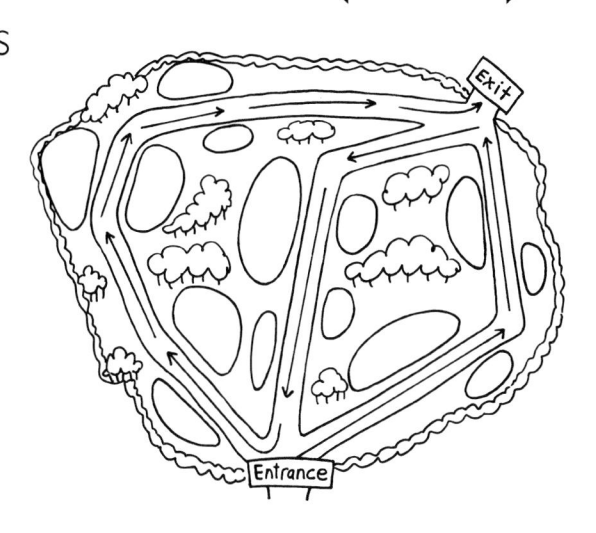

© TTS Group Ltd, 2012

CARD 97 : **Puzzling families** — PROBLEM

There are 3 families, and each family has 1 child. 2 of the children are girls, Angie and Rita, and the third is a boy, Roy. The mothers' names are Helen, Lily and Sue. The fathers' names are Eric, Frank and Allan. Here is what we know about the families:

1. Eric's daughter and Lily's daughter are members of a tennis club.
2. Frank's daughter is not called Angie.
3. Allan and Sue are not from the same family.

Do you know which 3 people belong in each family?

© TTS Group Ltd, 2012

CARD 97 : **Puzzling families** — SOLUTION

Because Lily and Eric each have a daughter, they cannot be in the same family. Frank also has a daughter. So he will be in the same family as Lily. As their daughter is not Angie, she must be Rita. So the first family is Frank, Lily and Rita.

As Sue and Allan are not from the same family, Sue must be in the same family as Eric. They have a daughter so she must be Angie. Now we know the second family: Eric, Sue and Angie.

Then we can easily work out the third family: Allan, Helen and Roy.

© TTS Group Ltd, 2012

CARD 98 : **Not in our club** PROBLEM

There are 26 children in the class. 10 of them belong to the chess club. 14 of them belong to the drama club. 5 of them belong to both.

How many children in the class don't belong to either club?

CARD 98 : **Not in our club** SOLUTION

7 children don't belong to either club.

If no one belonged to both clubs, we could find out the number of people who don't belong to either by taking away the number in the chess club and the number in the drama club from the total number in the class. However, 5 people belong to both clubs. When we work out 26 – 10 – 14, we take away those 5 people twice. So we need to add 5 on to get the correct answer: 26 – 10 – 14 = 2, then 2 + 5 = 7.

CARD 99: **What are the 3 numbers?** — PROBLEM

The product of 3 numbers is 120. The sum of the 2 smaller numbers is equal to the biggest number.

What are the 3 numbers?

CARD 99: **What are the 3 numbers?** — SOLUTION

The 3 numbers are 3, 5 and 8.

As the product of the 3 numbers is 120, they can be one of the following combinations: 1, 10, 12; 2, 6, 10; 2, 5, 12; 2, 3, 20; 3, 4, 10; 3, 5, 8; or 4, 5, 6. Among these possibilities, only 3, 5 and 8 can be the right choice because the sum of the smaller numbers (3 and 5) is the equal to the big number (8).

CARD 100: **The missing weight** — PROBLEM

Caitlin, Mikayla and Ben have packed up some sweets to post to their friends. Caitlin's package contains 3 chocolate bars, 7 lollipops and 1 packet of jelly beans. Mikayla's package contains 4 chocolate bars, 10 lollipops and 1 packet of jelly beans. Ben's package contains 1 chocolate bar, 1 lollipop and 1 packet of jelly beans.

Caitlin's package weighs 5.6 kilograms and Mikayla's weighs 6.8 kilograms. Can you figure out how much Ben's package weighs?

© TTS Group Ltd, 2012

CARD 100: **The missing weight** — SOLUTION

Ben's package weighs 3.4 kilograms. Caitlin has 2 more chocolate bars and 6 more lollipops than Ben. Mikayla has 1 more chocolate bar and 3 more lollipops than Caitlin, which comes to another 1.2 kilograms. That means 2 chocolate bars and 6 lollipops weigh 2.4 kilograms. So the weight of Caitlin's package (5.8 kilograms) take away 2.4 kilograms is the weight of Ben's package.

© TTS Group Ltd, 2012

CARD 101 : **Take away 1 matchstick**   PROBLEM

Take away 1 matchstick to make the two sides equal.

$$271 - 721 = 177 + 22$$

CARD 101 : **Take away 1 matchstick** SOLUTION

It is clear that including the number 721 makes it impossible to get a correct answer. One option is to change 721 into a two-digit number. You can't make a two-digit number by taking away 7 or 2 because you would need to take away more than 1 matchstick. So the only choice is to take away the number 1 from 721. Then we can find the correct answer:

$$271 - 72 = 177 + 22$$

CARD 102 : **Time to meet** — PROBLEM

Lily and Helen live 900 metres away from each other. Lily walks at a speed of 30 metres per minute. Helen walks at a speed of 60 metres per minute.

If they each start from their own home at 9.00 am and walk towards each other's home, at what time will they meet?

© TTS Group Ltd, 2012

CARD 102 : **Time to meet** — SOLUTION

They will meet at 9.10 am. As Helen walks twice as fast as Lily, the distance Lily walks + the distance Helen walks (twice the distance Lily walks) = 900 metres when they meet. That means Lily has walked for 300 metres, which will take her 10 minutes.

© TTS Group Ltd, 2012